Tina Sederholm is a poet ar
'Completely spellbinding' ****
***** (Three Weeks), she ha
theatre shows that have toure
the Edinburgh Fringe. A sought-after hea...
and spoken word circuit, she has performed everywhere ...
allotments to the Royal Albert Hall.

She also loves to help other writers hone their craft, providing
editing expertise through one to one mentoring and workshops.
When she is not writing or performing, Tina can be found walking
her dogs across the rolling North Oxfordshire landscape where
she lives. Formerly a successful event rider, trainer and author
of three books on equestrianism, she has also been known to
still give the odd riding lesson.

This is Not Therapy is her second full-length poetry collection.

This Is Not Therapy

Tina Sederholm

Burning Eye

BurningEyeBooks
Never Knowingly
Mainstream

This edition published by Burning Eye Books 2021

www.burningeye.co.uk

@burningeyebooks

Burning Eye Books
15 West Hill, Portishead, BS20 6LG

ISBN 978-1-913958-01-5

This Is Not Therapy

To the strong women in my family: Diana, Annalisa, Annika

CONTENTS

To Tina of the Early Nineties   11

REBRANDING GOD
The First Time I Came   14
Jesus Loves You   16
Vegetarian Special at the Horse and Groom   17
The Pope Wore Prada   19
Everything Is Sacred   20
Read Hitchhiker's!   22

TO PARENT OR NOT TO PARENT
Memo to Mothers   26
In the End You Have to Say It   28
For Those Who Are Not Mothers   29
Purgatory   30
Make Time for Family at Christmas   32

SLAVES WITH THE ILLUSION OF FREEDOM
How I Met Your Father   34
Life Choices   35
Woman's Search for Peace   37
Power of Attorney   39

IT'S ALL THERAPY
This Is for the Children Carrying Secrets   42
What's It All For?   43
Hearing Voices   45

WE CAME TO CREATE
This Is Not Therapy   48
Resistance Is Useless   49

The Artist as an Apprentice 51
Paterson 52

GHOST SHIPS
Palimpsest 56
Ghosts 57
Sometimes You Are So Far From Home 59

TINY JOYS AND EVERYDAY GURUS
The Universe Sent Us a Removal Man
Who Looks Like John Hegley 62
The Life-Changing Magic of Tidying 63
Give Me Cheese 64
Preaching to the Converted 65
Sunday Dog Walk 66
Marc Maron 67
Revelation 68
Some Good News 69

SOMEONE ELSE'S SHOES
For Hollie, Should She Need It 72
Dear Katie Hopkins 74
Anyone Could Be Arthur 77

EVERYTHING IS WORKING OUT
I Never Meant to Be a Poet 80
Earlier Reports of My Flaws Have Been
Exaggerated 83
Thank You. No, Thank You.
No, Thank You. 85
Look! at How I Am Held 87
How to Keep Going 89

TO TINA OF THE EARLY NINETIES

The first thing I want you to know
is the posturing, the pout,
the ache to be different,
the effort to win *the wittiest comment
at the table* competition
is going to end with a crash.

You are smacking your head against a brick wall
and the wall won't budge.
Bruised, blood-battered, bludgeoned,
you will be left with who you are.
Not the version you wished for.

You will not marry the man with a fortune
so you never have to think about money again.
You will have some forgettable sex.
And some terrible sex.
The man you do marry will not neutralise
the discomfort of being you.

Which is how you will learn to take care of yourself,
not make it someone else's career.
You will cease to flail in a swathe of hysteria,
like a Victorian in her gut-pinching corset
contorting her into a shape she was never meant to be.

In short, you will grow up.
You are not quite beautiful enough
to be rescued, thank God.
Anyone can be talented and gorgeous.
Kindness. That takes effort.
Especially with annoying people.

You are still unique.
No one else can screw up in quite the manner you can,
and now you have the freedom to do so.

Leave other people to screw up
in their particular way too.
It is not your business how they run their lives.

Promise to become unutterably yourself.
It will make you shiver.
But I guarantee you'll never be bored.

REBRANDING GOD

THE FIRST TIME I CAME

was courtesy of Jeffrey Archer.
All it took was the privacy
of my own bedroom,
a moderately well-written sex scene,
and an extra-thick Pentel marker pen.

Until then my sex education
had been strictly clinical.
No mention of the female orgasm;
the male one solely
for procreation.
How that fire was lit
consigned to the same bin
as any notion
of my own divinity.
These were skilfully eradicated
in a class named Divinity
and replaced
with the ongoing status
of sinner,
as if by traversing puberty
I had committed a crime.

I understood I should spend
the rest of my life,
head bowed,
atoning for my filthy existence,
and if I said all the right prayers,
there was a small chance
I might be forgiven.

Forgive me if I find this ridiculous.
Any deity that invented the clitoris
knew they were playing with fire.
I am more than halfway

through that filthy existence
and still wrestle with ideas of divinity,

but if I am to have a god,
they will permit, no, revel
in the pulse of engorged swelling.
Delight in the petals of her fiery furnace,
gasp at the lightning bolts
of love's sweet lava,
and embrace every magnificent
passion-moistened cliché,

even those courtesy
of Jeffrey Archer's pen.

JESUS LOVES YOU

I'm seven years old and dressed as Pocahontas. My schoolfriend Matthew is John Wayne and his mother is walking us to a Cowboys and Indians party. (Yes, I know. It was the seventies.) Matthew swaggers down the pavement, firing his pistol. As his mother and I pause at a pedestrian crossing, he bolts across the road without looking.

His mother shouts, *Jesus saw you do that!*

I can still feel my little body tighten up. I was already concerned about the see-everything-at-once God, and this incident proved my fear was well founded. I wasn't sure what Jesus was going to do with that information, but I imagined he had a giant abacus and had just moved one bead to the left on Matthew's row. A strike against Matthew's chances of getting into Heaven.

As I get older, I remain vigilant about how I behave in front of my invisible judge. After I get out of the bath, for instance, I take great care to dry in between my toes properly. I add school staff to the judging crew, specifically my maths teacher, Mrs Brownsword. I imagine God, Jesus and Mrs Brownsword crouched around a TV screen, analysing my drying technique, and my attempts to pick up my towel with my toes to correct my flat feet. This, even before I have read *Nineteen Eighty-Four*.

But the way I dried my feet would have made no difference to Mrs Brownsword or Jesus. The only place their judgment existed was in my head.

I'm sure Matthew's mother loved him and, scared he might get run over, came out with the biggest threat she could imagine, to frighten him into submission. But it's a strange kind of love that tries to protect people by threatening them.

I wonder what Jesus thinks when he sees us do that.

VEGETARIAN SPECIAL AT THE HORSE AND GROOM

They spelt it *Le Sagne*
on the pub specials board.
That's *L*, *E*, space, *Sagne*.
I shouldn't laugh;
after all, people in Britain
pronounce it that way.

But I can't help myself.
I keep saying *Le Sagne*,
laying the stress
on different syllables,
pompous arse that I am
after a couple glasses of red.

And it doesn't get boring
to repeat *Le SAGne, Le SagNE,
Le Le Le Sagne*!

These tiny errors happen so easily.
Imagine in the Bible,
if *t'shuvah* had been better translated.
Instead of *repent*,
the scribe had found a word
closer to the original Aramaic return.
Then we would not need to repent our sins,
only *return* from them.
Like reversing out of a cul-de-sac
when the satnav gets confused.

Maybe it was a bad day.
Maybe the scribe's bowels ached
after a confrontation
with his brother,
and, carrying

certain judgments
on how some people should behave,
he felt his brother could do more
to earn forgiveness.
Thought, *Sod it.*
Repent will do.

Maybe the scribe at the chalkboard in the pub
was having a similar moment.
Remembered being ridiculed in French class
as they dithered between le and la
and, having never studied Italian,
thought, *Well… it sounds like a le.*

I ordered *Le Sagne* anyway.
The point is: it was delicious.
Tomatoes from the pub garden,
homemade béchamel,
a sprig of parsley cut not ten minutes before.

Perhaps it is a universal truth,
whether considering lasagne or a bible:
one should seek a little deeper
and always check out the source.

THE POPE WORE PRADA

Pope Benedict XVI removes his red Gucci shoes for the last time.

Farewell, ruby slippers.
I'm heading back to Kansas;
turns out being Dorothy
wasn't all it was cracked up to be.
I clicked my heels as best I could,
but too often the Wizard was sleeping.

Scarecrow, Lion, Tin Man,
we had some great times:
sips of communion wine,
praying until sunrise.
True, there is no place like Rome,
but home is where I'm headed.

I was never meant to be a politician,
the bloodied feet of Christ
was not a look that worked for me,
and eighty-nine is too old to pretend
to be anything but a professor.
My life will end in brown brogues;
how easily my feet slip in.

EVERYTHING IS SACRED

Even you, a beechwood coffee table,
sickly as a Dickensian orphan.
Peculiar in your stillness,
your perfectly planed edges
breathe neither in nor out.
Stripped of your bark,
function, now your identity.

It seems a great fatigue
has come over you.
If you had eyes,
they would be glazed.
I want to paint you,
go crazy with a spray can,
karate-chop your legs,
leave scars that say
you were once at the party.

Somewhere beneath your varnish,
redolent of a grey suit
bought off the rack at Next,
there is still the faintest heartbeat.
This is not what you meant to become:
something I am free to put a hot mug on,
because you are only Ikea.

As you descend the career ladder,
sold on eBay or collected for charity,
you might salvage one last gasp
when classed as charmingly retro,
until smashed up by drunk students.

Find yourself in pieces –
perhaps as a shelf in a mildewed shed –
wondering what it was all in aid of,
before a quiet funeral

on a forgotten corner of landfill.

READ HITCHHIKER'S!

The impulse came urgently,
unexpected. Like a surprised sperm
whale suspended above an alien planet.
Or a bowl of petunias.

Douglas would have chuckled at the irony
of divine inspiration, or God, if you wish,
reminding me to reread a book
that disproved God, or rather,
replaced it with a computer
called Deep Thought.
Which, if you think about it,
is another metaphor
for the metaphor called God.

I applaud those people
who type *G-d*.
They are at least trying to grasp
the ungraspable.
That vaporous notion
that there is something bigger than these bodies.
Although G-d falls sadly short.

Reading a book about a book emblazoned
with the words *Don't Panic* on the cover
is the perfect antidote to a pandemic.
A book that points out, time and again,
that nothing is what we assume.
That embracing the improbable
can take you anywhere,
whereas an answer is kind of the end of the road.

Call this unnameable whatever you want:
energy, world, love, grace, kindness,
call it Nigel.
I'm not saying you have to believe
in Nigel.

I don't want to either,
certainly not the way I was taught.

Yet I can't help
but stare into space
more often than I should,
overwhelmed
by what is common, everyday
and powerful about all of us.

TO PARENT OR NOT TO PARENT

MEMO TO MOTHERS

This is a reminder
that you are Head of Department
in the largest, most complex
and vital organisation in the world.

Specifically, you are in charge
of the people who will ensure
the continued success
of this organisation.

Every day you negotiate peace
between warring factions.
Haggle over contracts,
keep your end of the bargain
and make sure everyone
gets to bed, clean, fed
and with the correct teddy bear
in their possession.

You mastermind crisis meetings,
fundraisers, dinners.
On any given morning you can whip up
a Willy Wonka or Fantastic Mr Fox outfit
in less than five minutes.
Everyone in the company has the freedom
to explore their creativity, knowing
you will scoop the mess up afterwards.

Forgive me if I get het up sometimes.
I wish you'd stop trying
to maintain invincibility
and invisibility simultaneously.
I wish you'd realise it is impossible
to pay you an adequate wage.
I wish you'd realise
there is no point waiting

for others to notice.
Your children will only thank you
at some indeterminate point
in a far-off future.

They're so lucky you don't
just drop everything.
But you wouldn't.
You never let this department down,
and the only person who thinks otherwise
is yourself.

In this matter, you are wrong.
You will have to take it from me
that without you,
the world would actually stop.

You are Head of Department
in the largest, most complex
and vital organisation in the world,
and sometimes the responsibility breaks you.

Let it. There is an even stronger person
waiting inside to emerge.
A woman you had no idea
you could become.

IN THE END YOU HAVE TO SAY IT

People are always losing things.
Glasses, pens, socks. Those purple mittens
your granny knitted. Babies.

They fall down the back of sofas,
get left on trains, in car parks. On Tuesdays,
in the starched pistachio of a hospital room.

People are always losing things,
and somewhere these items are filed
or shredded. Recycled or incinerated.

This someone struggles to recall
the former self who hung the laundry,
who won last night's game of Scrabble

still spread upon the table.
Who knew what she'd be doing
late September.

This someone has no clue at all.
She puts her left foot in front of her right,
relieved when they hit what feels

like solid ground.

FOR THOSE WHO ARE NOT MOTHERS

When that (straight, white, male) comedian commented
that women are amazing because they make all of the
people
and produce the most nourishing food for all of those
people,
I thought, *Yeah!*
But the word snagged in my throat,
because I am not one of those women.

He doesn't know that when I lost my first,
the woman who stroked my face
as I came round from the operation
was neither my mother
nor had ever given birth,

yet mothered me when I needed it most.
He doesn't know how featherlike,
how necessary her touch was,
how I kept my eyes closed long after I was conscious
because I didn't want the stroking to stop.

It was sweet of that comedian to at least notice mothers.
He should expose his feelings more.
Vulnerability looks good on a man.

PURGATORY

Summer barbecue.
A glass and a half of wine,
enough to feel woozily
at one with the world,
when a six-year-old asks,
So. Where do dead people go?

And she's staring at me
with a saucer-eyed smile
and I know
I'm about to lie
because what I want to say
is, Heaven? That's just a concept.
A best guess,
a get-out-of-jail-free card
designed to justify suffering
by reckoning
there's something better
around the corner.
A place where pain isn't.
Where there's no fighting
or killing, unlike Earth,
where we principally kill each other
over which version of God
guarantees entrance into Heaven,
a concept which may or may not exist.

But even the atheists
around the table
are silently pleading with me
to stick with the programme.
They may not believe in God,
but they do believe
in a six-year-old's right
to a state of bliss.

I still want to tell her
Heaven is a concept,
a best guess
to make up for the mess
we live in.
And just because
some people believe
this idea
doesn't make it true.

When what I should say is
I don't know.
I don't know
where dead people go.
All I know is
they were here,
now they're not,
and the bit that has gone
must have gone somewhere.
And the fact Aunty Freda
left behind the body she used to wear
may be proof that she was more
than that body,
and if she was more than
her body,
then I am more than this body,
this age, this hairstyle,
these genitals.

The six-year-old waits.
She wants a definitive answer
and I mustn't knock adults
off their pedestal just yet.

So I cut her some cake
and tell her a story.
I at least have the courage
to make it a good one.

MAKE TIME FOR FAMILY AT CHRISTMAS

My sister asks me to buy
an alarm clock for my nephew.
He's having trouble
learning to tell the time
in a house filled
with laptops and iPhones.

I am relieved.
The world of little boys
is a mystery to me
and this is a gift of an idea,

but, standing in a shop,
faced with an array of clocks,
my stomach turns, giddy
with my first memories of helplessness.
Dragged to a car
because it was time to go.
Handcuffed to an adult's schedule
of when to eat, play, sleep. Cry.

I buy him the clock anyway.
On Christmas night
he stumbles downstairs.
Face swollen with fatigue,
he asks Mum to take the clock away.
He can't sleep
because it won't stop ticking.

SLAVES WITH THE ILLUSION OF FREEDOM

HOW I MET YOUR FATHER

My parents met at a party in the early sixties. My father noticed my mother because she tipped a full punch bowl over a chinless wonder who was attempting to chat her up.

While they were dancing, my father said, *You would be alright if you got your head out of the clouds.*

Over dinner on their first date, he tells her,

Horses should be slaves with the illusion of freedom.
And so should wives.

My mother replies,

But who's the one with the illusion?

The jury is still out on that one.

LIFE CHOICES

Rebecca's forearm is starring in a commercial.
After four hours in wardrobe, the arm is presented
to the company marketing team.
They stroke their chins.
We're not sure lilac is the colour for today.

No one quite knows what they mean
and the preliminary shots have already been taken,
so, like it or not, lilac is the colour for today.
But before the director can proceed,
the liquidologist clears his throat.

He has poured a precise amount of cream liqueur
into a glass that he previously polished
to an ephemeral sheen.
Now he asks, *Should the ice cubes
be consciously present, or unconsciously present?*
The company, he says, *prefer consciousness,*
but today's producer *leans the other way.*

Rebecca's forearm's co-star, a husky-cross-boxer,
is a consummate professional.
A direct correlation between tapping his paw
on a keyboard and the appearance of a liver treat
means he is clear about his direction,
but even he takes exception when the glass
balanced on his head slides off,
smashes to the ground.

After three years at RADA –
her Lady Macbeth found noteworthy –
Rebecca mithers about this career decision,
but her forearm is sulking.
Sniffs that being paid
for something ridiculous
is preferable to no payment at all.

When Rebecca continues to fret,
her forearm gives her the finger.
Threatens to leave
and find its own agent.

WOMAN'S SEARCH FOR PEACE

My inner PA believes
I will achieve inner peace
by finishing every item
on my to-do list.
Like the promise
of a pot of gold
at the end of a rainbow,
my PA is sold on the idea
that I will only find peace
at the end of a list,
which means there is no peace
until the list is done.

But the list is never done,
because the end of one to-do list
always produces another one.

And another one.

And another…

And a sub-list,
broken into action steps,
one of which is
to make a master
list of lists.

Imagine if I did reach
the end of every list.
World saved, shows made,
books written, accounts balanced,
house more spotless than a show room…

Then what?
Left with nothing to do,
I'd have to write

a notes for future generations list,
a please don't forget me list,
a what to do when I'm dead list.

Because I bet I'll still get emails
after I'm gone.
I'll be on Vision Direct's list
for a reminder every three months
to order contact lenses
and no one will know how to cancel it
because you're not supposed
to make a passwords list.

Some days I can't do the list.
But the list still produces
another one

and another
and another

and there is no peace
because

- The list is never done.
- The list is never done.
- The list is never done.

Oh.
Oh.
Ohhh.

POWER OF ATTORNEY

My father says he can see horses
out of the hospital window.
We are on the sixth floor.
All I can see are treetops.

He grapples with his catheter,
fiddles with the drip in his hand.
Why don't we go home?

I tell him he hasn't been able to eat
for a week, legs too wobbly
to hold him up.

You're in hospital, I say.
Ah, he says, *in Sweden.*
Like Sweden, I say, *but Oxford.*

We watch the rain beat on the window.
Competitions cancelled this weekend, I say.
Yes, he says. *Now go and fetch those horses in.*

IT'S ALL THERAPY

THIS IS FOR THE CHILDREN CARRYING SECRETS

Especially those dressed in suits,
who create elegant spreadsheets
and always hand reports in on time,
yet feel like the lame child left behind
when the Pied Piper played his flute.

This is for the children carrying secrets,
whose memories are fractured
by fragments that don't fit.
Who feel unaccountably sick
when a friend recommends a novel
about Nicaraguan street kids.

And this is for the children
who don't know they are carrying secrets,
whose mantras are:
It wasn't that bad.
Nothing really happened.

Yet gabble in nightmares,
wear their bruises like rosebuds,
lose themselves in wardrobes,
not looking for Narnia
but the certainty of walls.

The children who thought
it was up to them to fix the leak,
who grew up long ago,
but still drag a teddy bear behind them.
Who say,
It wasn't that bad.
Nothing really happened.

WHAT'S IT ALL FOR?

Not long after he received his lung cancer diagnosis and subsequent estimate of six months to live, my father-in-law turned to me and asked, *What was it all for?*

We were walking to the chip shop. A closed man, face as weathered as a tree stump, Alan could huff louder than his beloved steam trains when asked to lay the table or move his shoes. These tiny journeys we would take together were a chance for him to tell me things no one else in the family knew.

This question felt like a cry from the heart. For the latter part of his working life, Alan had risen at 3.30am to drive HGVs, after surviving near-bankruptcy when his garden shed business went bust in the mid-nineties. Pam, his wife, had been diabetic all her life and 'died' on the operating table when being treated for a thyroid issue. A heart attack in 2000 left her depressed and unable to drive. Now she had dementia. Spent most of her day in front of the TV, continually turning the volume up and down. Alan had taken care of her and been through the usual dramas: falling out with family members over petty disagreements and slights. Losing his dad suddenly and his mother slowly.

I couldn't answer his question. He had rarely seemed a happy man, except when building his model railway. His sister once mentioned a holiday in Tunisia when Alan had drunk a local spirit – a rare occurrence – and had briefly accepted a belly dancer's invitation to join her on stage. *He actually laughed*, she said. It had been some time in the eighties.

And now, facing death, he asked, *What was it all for?*

Maybe it was even more of a cry to me, because I've always had a latent terror of wasting my life. What if I get to the end and realise I've got it wrong? It's a question that bears down

43

on me in the early hours more often than I care to mention. I want the opposite. I want to get to the end of my life and say, *That was great.*

When I began learning to craft stories, I discovered the Hero's Journey, Joseph Campbell's theory that stories across all cultures share the same underlying structure. An individual is called to adventure, goes through various trials and obstacles and eventually receives his prize. Think Indiana Jones, Luke Skywalker, the knights of the Round Table, Frodo, Dorothy.

The reason we love these stories so much, according to Campbell, is because this structure echoes the passage of our own lives, the same journey we all must take for self-realisation, spiritual growth and fulfilment.

For a long time I thought that the point of the Hero's Journey was the big win, the shiny object. Boy gets girl. Knight finds Holy Grail. Woman gets home. Sheriff kills shark.

As a result, every time I've failed, whether it's not getting a gig, winning a prize, landing a job or sticking to a diet, I feel fatally deficient in some way. Wasting my life.

One day I read that the point of the Hero's Journey was not the prize. The point was the healing they received along the way. The lost parts of themselves that they rediscovered in the trials and tribulations of the journey. In any case, the heroes don't get to keep the prize. The Knights have to release the Holy Grail. Frodo doesn't keep the ring. Moses never enters the Promised Land. Indy doesn't keep the Ark. Lyra can't stay with Will. Rick gives up Ilsa.

I wish Alan was still here, so I could tell him that. As it was, the last words I whispered in his ear were, *It's okay to let go.*

We were leaving his hospital bed and I could see he was agitated by the fuss other people were making. He didn't have the strength left to make it better for anyone. He slipped away in the middle of the night, a week or so later. No one around. I'll hazard a guess that's the ending he wanted.

HEARING VOICES

I once met a man who became
so angry with his hands
he thrust them in petrol
and lit a match.

They mostly melted.
On the right, his forefinger
and part of the second remained;
the other, a shiny, pinked
stump with no thumb.
He was left with a choice:
hold a cigarette, or light one
for someone else.

Mostly, he wore mittens
and avoided picking things up in public.
At least I have one claw left, he said,
to keep scratching at the world.

Mostly, you should listen to people
with the sound turned down.
That way, you can spot the lazy flies
wandering out of their mouths.
They don't mean to lie,
but their twitches and glances
betray the stories they sold
themselves as truth.

Truths usually arrive as a whisper.
Write yours down before they fade like dreams
or flatten into an everyday drone.
Otherwise they will grieve for years,
bury themselves in migraines.
Spill out of your eyes
when your favourite character dies
in *The Wire. Breaking Bad. Killing Eve.*

WE CAME TO CREATE

THIS IS NOT THERAPY

Ha!
As if we don't constantly daub
that wound with Sudocrem.
Try to keep a plaster on it.

As if every moment we don't ache
to be understood. To be heard.
Always grasping to feel better,
even when the method is suspect.
Why else have *one more for the road*?

I used to believe my parents had all the answers,
but as my mother glimpses her eighties
without a husband, she asks,
How do I do this bit?

and I realise I am not the only one
who makes it up as she goes along.
Besieged by the desire for a story
that makes sense of the world.

Or at least one scrawled sentence
that encourages the edges
to knit back together.

RESISTANCE IS USELESS

You know how it is. You wake one morning, as the light is edging round the curtains, before the drone of traffic begins to gnaw at your brain, and you know, with a stone-cold certainty, that life is short, people are dying and you need to do that thing that whispers to you in the quiet moments. Doesn't matter if it is creating art or starting a business or merely painting the downstairs loo. You need to start it now.

So you organise childcare, husbandcare, cancel... whatever. Today is the day. But what do you find yourself doing at the allotted hour? Scrolling through Facebook? Putting one more basket of washing away? Calling window cleaners, checking up on that friend because... well, that's what good people do. Anything but the longing you promised to attend to this morning.

I used to doubt my decision to be a writer several times a day. The days I didn't revel in doubt, I distracted myself by disliking my day job and falling in love with unsuitable men. You know. The usual stuff.

The doubt made me question my desires. I loved the idea of being a writer, but I could indulge in epic resistance dances around the act of writing. I couldn't write today because I was too tired/too upset/something else needed dealing with/ someone had pissed me off... what an imagination. This had me confused. Surely, if I did everything to avoid the thing I purported to love, this must mean I didn't really love it. I was kidding myself.

I was in one of these sloughs of despond when I got a chance to work with a FAMOUS POET. I was a member of a women's group in an online coaching forum. The leader announced she was going to run an in-person retreat in four months' time, which would include working with the FAMOUS POET. I love this FAMOUS POET. It was his writing that drew me back to poetry in my thirties after abandoning it many years before.

I wanted to go to that retreat. But it was in America, and I was pretty broke at the time. Luckily, help was on its way. The ladies in the group started cheerleading for me. We brainstormed ways to create extra income. I rang a friend in the States I hadn't seen for years, who said he would collect me from the airport and drive me to the retreat in Charleston. I got new clients, worked weekends, lost a stone in weight because I cut out meat from my diet to save money. I worked in subzero temperatures with Asda bags lining my boots because they were leaking and I didn't want to spend money on new ones.

I got there.

The FAMOUS POET is well known for asking beautiful and challenging questions. The question that got me was:

What brings you most alive? By simply being in contact with it, you take on a grace that you don't usually have.

I sat in this former church, felt my answer echo off the vaulted ceiling.

Writing and performing, of course.

No other calling for me. Nothing with better career prospects or a regular income. My resistance wasn't a sign I was indulging in the wrong vocation. In fact, it was a diagnostic that I was exactly where I was meant to be.

This came as both a relief and a disappointment.

THE ARTIST AS AN APPRENTICE

After my attempt to emulate the advice of the sculptor
Rodin to the young poet Rilke: to find an animal at the
Jardin des Plantes and watch it until he couldn't help but
write about it.

Today I am arguing with trees.
I want them to grow at speed,
so I can watch them unfold.
I want to witness a leaf
bursting free, but, so sneaky,
they only sprout buds
when my back is turned.

Why so secretive?
Placid and implacable,
the trees don't answer.
Stand their ground
as the most hooligan of winds
rips branches from their grasp.

Until the moment they don't.
When, with a great crack
in the shroud of night,
uncaring of would-be witnesses,
they crash to the ground.

Even then, their limbs
become art against the sky.
The bastards.
And, though indifferent
to the statement they make,

beneath their bark,
I'm sure I can hear
laughter.

PATERSON

I watched the film *Paterson* last night.
Having gorged on Netflix dramas
for many months, I found myself

squirming on the sofa,
willing something to happen.
Willing someone to get shot.

But Paterson is a bus driver
whose route never changes.
Nor his routine of writing poems

moments before leaving the depot,
in a notebook propped against the steering wheel
or whilst eating a sandwich in the park.

Eventually a guy did pull a gun
in a bar, though it wasn't important
to the overall story, such as it was.

I did appreciate the beauty
of *Jarmusch*'s composition,
the way the light fell in every scene.

I became calmed by the dailiness of it all.
How everyone you meet is a poet
when they pause long enough,

and at the end
something small but significant,
involving a bulldog, did occur.

Next morning I walk my own dog
on my usual route through the woods.
Blossom frees itself from branches

and for the first time in months
I hear a poem, fully formed,
clear as the wind converses with trees.

GHOST SHIPS

PALIMPSEST

Last night I dreamt I was dreaming of you
and woke with a yearning that comes
from the rousing of the unresolved,
a crime filed but never solved, the one
that irks the detective until his final day.
Old alibis have become the source
of minor legends, but, despite fine efforts
to merge myself with other stories,
abstinence has not quietened the deep
low throb of original evidence:
fingerprints from a kindred life,
the one where everything
clearly worked out for the best.

GHOSTS

These are the stables
where my ponies used to live.
Now a kitchen –
no ring ties or mangers –
though the rug racks
high on the back wall
make an interesting feature.

I show my husband
where we stacked hay,
the outline of a stable door
in the dining room wall.
It used to stick, I tell him.
You had to hitch it with your hip
as you slid the bolt.

He nods like an obedient tourist,
then leaves to find beer.
I am rooted in footprints
owned by a previous self
he will never know,
a girl who hung rosettes on that wall,
hosed her ponies down
on this bit of concrete,
shampooed their tails
while dressed in a bikini.

My friend has made this her home.
She dances round the kitchen
in a silver sequinned dress;
her still-slim legs
end in pixie boots.
But our jawlines are cushiony;
both will take a day or two
to recover from that third bottle.

My feet dance with her,
but my heart leans back,
remembers the promise
I apprenticed myself to,
mucking out these stables
every day at dawn.
That anything was possible.

I didn't know that anything
would be this.

SOMETIMES YOU ARE SO FAR FROM HOME

all you can do
is name all the ways you've strayed.

Sometimes all you can say
is exactly how exhausted you are,
how sick of small talk, applications, jumping through hoops.

You only took your eyes from the road
for a moment or two,
and suddenly years have passed

since you last looked your love in the eye.
And it was always for excellent reasons,
a couple of months at most.

Sometimes all you have to do
is name all the ways
you've tried to escape.

How deep your cravings are.
How your hunger could eat you alive.

You don't have to forgive yourself.
Today, it is enough to no longer answer,
Fine, to the question, *How are you?*

Instead you will say, *Not okay.*
This is not okay.

The first step towards
a life you could call your own.

TINY JOYS AND EVERYDAY GURUS

THE UNIVERSE SENT US A REMOVAL MAN
WHO LOOKS LIKE JOHN HEGLEY

Or not John Hegley exactly,
but his mardy older brother.

No mandolin, but he does peer
school teacher-esquely
over wire-rimmed glasses
as he views the contents
of our shed.

Huffs at the marriage
of our scoliotic stairs
and my antique pedestal desk,
much as John sighs
and shakes his head
at an audience who refuse
to sit in the front row.

But the plastic record storage cases
elicit a quiver from a corner
of his mouth. He admits
to being a fan of punk,
and with a heave of his shoulders

acquiesces to our ambitious estimate
of *not owning all that much,*

as John might forgive
a small child in a workshop
for misinterpreting his instructions.

THE LIFE-CHANGING MAGIC OF TIDYING

Marie Kondo told me
socks need to breathe
when they are not at work.

I never considered
my socks might have a life
outside me.

That they might get depressed
if squashed together
like commuters on a train

or avocados vacuum-packed
all the way from Peru.

That they might prefer
to meditate
like tiny woolly buddhas

or coil like cats,
breathe the healing balm
of sleep through their fibres,

preparing for the moment
I need them to be friends
to my feet again.

I owe them this.
Socks can't take antidepressants,
drink away a bad day.

They can only send distress signals
through threadbare heels
and frayed elastic.

GIVE ME CHEESE

Ralph has trained me
to give him a treat
every time he runs to my side.

He has perfected the wide-eyed
dreamy look guaranteed
to push my hand into my pocket.

He often returns before I've whistled,
safe in the knowledge
that I will retrieve cheese, bacon rind, a biscuit.

I find I do not mind
that I have been trained
in this way.

We have become those
who know each other
far too well.

A comfort against
our failure to excel
in our local obedience class.

PREACHING TO THE CONVERTED

Yet again this month
the parish magazine implores
residents with dogs
to pick up their poo.

Suggested strategies include:
keeping the dog close
even when off lead,
looking behind you regularly,
teaching the youth
(the problem is always worse in the holidays)

to use the free poo bags
distributed in handy containers
next to the forty-eight bins situated
around the village.

Dogs will continue to excrete.
People who do not read
the parish magazine
will continue to ignore
these nuggets of wisdom
or, on a good day, kick their shit
into the high grass.

SUNDAY DOG WALK

Eddie, my neighbour, says
that since I saw him on Thursday
he has successfully defrosted the freezer.

Though, when melted water
began to drip onto the travel hairdryer
he was using to finish the job,

he felt awkward
at his possible inclusion
in the book of unnecessary deaths,

his electrocuted corpse only discovered
when his partner returned from a work trip,
splayed over the lip of the chest freezer,

caught in a moment of indecision
about what to take out for dinner.

MARC MARON

They say *never meet your heroes*,
but after a gig that
I had just commented
was breathtakingly crafted
and delivered with an ease I long for,
we passed the stage door
as Marc Maron walked out.

Thank goodness I needed to use
the ladies' after the show
and that the queue
had been the exact length required
to facilitate this moment
is not what I said
as I shook Marc Maron's hand.

But what I enjoyed most
was the way Marc Maron didn't wait
for Neil to approach
but stepped towards him,
hand outstretched,

thus ending a seventeen-year loop
of disappointment, caused
by an underwhelming chance
encounter with Philip Glass.

REVELATION

It happens, of course, when you're on holiday.
Sat on a balcony,
you gaze over an ocean
laden with crystals,
while the first scent of bergamot
drifts off a teacup,
and in a slight forgetting of yourself
the muslin curtain floats up,
the horizon tilts
and you gasp. Breath flown.
Intoxicated by all manner of possibility.

Then you go home,
force yourself
to like, again, things
you don't care about.
Except that one day,
tan faded, vacant-eyed,
toiling around a supermarket,
you find yourself,
for no apparent reason,
picking up a packet of Earl Grey.

SOME GOOD NEWS

Lately, whenever I feel down, I think of the Afghan all-girls robotics team. I have many assumptions about what it might mean to be a woman growing up in Afghanistan. Assumptions of burkhas and early childbirth, rudimentary schooling and arranged marriages. So a team of girls who make robots from scrap metal and without protective equipment – because who's heard of health and safety when the Taliban are glowering outside? – amaze me.

Invited to compete at a robotics convention in America, they are twice refused visas, applications which involved 500-mile trips from their home city of Herat to the American embassy in Kabul. But they find someone to lobby Ivanka Trump, who puts in a good word with Dad, and he grants them admittance. Six Afghan Muslim women persuade Donald Trump to do something big-hearted. That's enough to make your head explode.

In America, they win medals at the convention for their solar-powered robots that seed fields. They dream of designing one to clear landmines.

Yes, they had parents who believe in educating females, though, when they return to Afghanistan, newspapers snipe that they've behaved immodestly, decreased their marriageability by wearing jeans. But they are women, and women the world over know that kind of story.

And they come from a city, not a rural village, but don't tell me that in every settlement everywhere there isn't at least one crone speaking her mind, giving men the necessary hell.

I may not be able to update my iPhone without assistance, but I resonate with these girls' ingenuity. I don't have the Taliban outside my door, but I feel a kinship with their resolute natures.

I am looking at a photo of the Afghan all-girls robotics team. They are smiling. And so am I.

SOMEONE ELSE'S SHOES

FOR HOLLIE, SHOULD SHE NEED IT

You who treat poetry as a religion,
believe that grace is only available
to the chosen few,

and the rest who don't follow the rules
should be expelled to the hell
of mediocrity:

I hear you.

After all, there are only so many awards
to go round, and those poets
who sing each other's praises,

claiming anyone can be a messiah,
need to be taught a thing or two.
Surely one requires a PhD

to feel the spark of the divine.
Should sacrifice many hours
to earn the right to call oneself poet.

How galling to discover
that even a homeless man
sitting on cardboard,

confessing that the love of his dog
gets him up in the morning,
reveals a lyrical wisdom.

That a woman
publishing her childhood poems
as part of a prizewinning collection

could be praised for bravery,
not castigated for an eight-year-old's lack
of academic rigour.

Go back to your scriptures.
Read what you held sacred
with fresh eyes.
Dig deeper.
There are churches enough
for everyone.

DEAR KATIE HOPKINS

I read your tweet to Tory peer Baroness Warsi
saying the Conservatives weren't her party;
they were 'our' party. You said we control the country now
and it's time to put British people first.

I wondered if you could clarify
a couple of points for me.
You see, my dad has Alzheimer's
and lives in a care home,
and it's bad, Katie.
Some days he can't stop crying
and Ibrahim is the only person
who can calm him down.
Then there's Sayeeda, Constantin, Tatiana…
and the nurse who changes Dad's colostomy bag,
she has the biggest smile.
I mean, it's so big Boris would comment on it.
Have you ever seen a colostomy bag explode,
Katie Hopkins?
Or, should I say, smelt a colostomy bag explode,
because the stench, it could melt concrete.
And while we're stuffing
our noses into our hands
so we don't gag, Twi…
well, I won't give you her whole name
because I don't want you to track her down –
she smiles and wipes down my dad, and the walls
and the bedding, and sings to him whilst she does it.

We had to put Dad in a home
because Mum got a brain tumour
and she couldn't look after Dad
and we couldn't manage the pair of them.
Do you know, not one of the specialists Mum saw
was what you would call British?
And none of the nursing staff;

well, there was one Scots woman,
but I guess she won't hang around long.

So I was just wondering, Katie Hopkins,
what's going to happen to people
who, according to you,
aren't strictly British.
Like my dad. He's Swedish,
and you wouldn't believe the trouble he had
arriving in Britain in the early fifties,
sounding like a German.

And if I'm honest, Katie Hopkins,
I'm a bit concerned for myself.
Where are you going to draw the line?
How British do I have to be to qualify?
I'm white, tick, born in Britain, tick,
I have a patrician forehead, tick,
but my dad is Swedish and I have this Jewish name.
Not that I am Jewish; it was my father's stepfather
who passed it on.
Will you take that into consideration
when you draw the line?
Because I look right,
but scratch a little,
it's another matter.

And I've just finished season three
of *The Man in the High Castle*,
you know, where the Nazis win the war,
and, given a few years,
you won't believe how far they go
to achieve racial purity.

I'm just a little bit immigrant.
Nothing worth mentioning
in the grand scale of things,
and I know how you feel about keeping
the talented ones,

but surely Baroness Warsi is one
of the talented ones,
so I'm a little confused.
Can you clarify?
Can you say where you'll draw the line?
Do I qualify?

Yours sincerely,
Tina Sederholm,
just a little bit immigrant.

ANYONE COULD BE ARTHUR

Imagine, on a Thursday morning,
your world doesn't fall apart;
it disappears.

Demolished. Gone.
Vomited into no kind of atmosphere,
you are bounced between stars,

teeth sucked down to your genitals
and back again, only to crash
into the longest open mic in history

with no MC to shout time
to those with a Vogon-inflated sense
of their own importance.

A fish in your ear translates
every excruciating word,
and enlightenment, it turns out,

isn't all it's cracked up to be.
Pushed out of another airlock,
time ties a bungee cord around your neck,

and you can't tell if you're laughing
because repetition is funny
or because you're hysterical.

You haven't ingested ayahuasca
with a Colombian shaman.
It's just shitting life.

Enough to blow your head off
and ram the immensity
of the universe into its space.

No amount of tea
will help you figure this out.

Come to think of it,
this could be any given Thursday.

EVERYTHING IS WORKING OUT

I NEVER MEANT TO BE A POET

There was no great love
of poetry in my family.
No sonnets at bedtime,
no Edward Lear.
The occasional limerick,
but the only poets I knew
were dead. Or Pam Ayres.

Aged eleven, our teacher told us
to compose a poem
about our favourite activity.
I chose riding a dressage test.
She commented beneath in red cursive,
Some interesting language
but I don't understand what you're talking about.
And I thought, *Yeah well,*
that definitely makes it a poem.

I never planned to study poetry,
but my first A-level essay was on wit in John Donne.
I wrote a fulsome and impassioned debate
on whether anybody had ever found
metaphysical poetry funny.
My teacher took me aside.
You missed the point, she said.
And I thought, *Well, that's because*
there is no point to poetry.

Soon after, I got my first gig.
Grandpa's funeral.
I shook the whole way through
my recitation of 'To the Horse'
by Ronald Duncan.
Funny how the words made
my voice tremor too.
The audience response was muted,

but afterwards
a great-uncle patted me on the arm,
said, *Well done up there.*

But I didn't have time to be a poet.
Too far into The Cure and Bauhaus.
Too busy lusting after pale, interesting
lost boys, but when they didn't lust back,
I wrote poems to an invisible audience
about how those boys got me so wrong.
Shame my best piece ended
with a Phil Collins couplet.

I managed to avoid poetry
for another ten years.
Still aiming for something more fur coats
and flash photography.
More podium finishes, possible Oscars,
a sixteen-page spread in *Hello* magazine,
and you don't get that for writing a few poems.

But when the trophy cabinet remained empty
and I wandered in the wilderness,
unable to choose any direction,
a friend handed me a tape of poetry,
and I sat in an ordinary park
in a nowhere suburb and listened
on my Sony Walkman.
Couldn't stop the tears,
though I only understood about thirty per cent.
In retrospect, that was good going.

Still, it took two years to write
three poems, and even longer to sneak
into my first open mic.
Shout my poem over the clank and hiss
of a cappuccino machine.
As I finished my final line,
I received from the audience

my first poetry… *ahhh*.
I had no idea how significant
that gasp was, but it felt good.
The first echo of home.

EARLIER REPORTS OF MY FLAWS HAVE BEEN EXAGGERATED

I've been looking at photos of myself
in my twenties. Those sinuous thighs!
The flatness of that stomach!

How I wished my breeches were 24 long,
not 26. Believed a pound of flesh
was one pound too many.

I wanted to stand out but stayed plain
so only the most astute man
would notice me.

He didn't.

But now in my fifties,
when there is no danger
in being beautiful,
beautiful is what I am.

My thighs may be cottage bloomers
rippling with braided curves,
but there is history here.

That ridge, possibly the result
of eating gelato on a beach all summer,
but why would I want to lose a memory like that?

The dent in my right quad,
a horse kicking me as I was on my phone:
a reminder that efficient multitasking is a fantasy.

My thighs are war heroines.
Roughly stitched back together
on the battlefield, they dance
the dance of survivors.

Their armour may be flesh,
but their resolve is ironclad.

THANK YOU. NO, THANK YOU.
NO, THANK YOU.

We got married in a friend's garden. I say *friend*; in fact, Maggie and I had only recently met on a writing course. Neil and I had lost our venue and, in a blurt of desperation and blind hope, I asked if anyone in the room had a garden we could use. Maggie said, *Come and see ours.*

It was just what we wished for: a couple of acres, partly formal, partly filled with a wild flower meadow, looking out across rolling Cotswold hills. Over coffee, Maggie said, *We don't have to stay friends forever because of this.*

Perfect. Just the sort of person I could be friends with, forever.

As a thank-you, we invited Maggie and her husband John to the post-wedding lunch we'd organised for friends who had stayed overnight. Neil and I were going to pay, but when the bill came, it had already been settled. One of our other friends had arranged for everyone to chip in their share.

Filled with that warm feeling that accompanies the knowledge that you have the best friends in the world, we were halfway to our honeymoon in the Lake District when we realised that meant Maggie and John must have paid for their thank-you meal.

Slicked with guilt, I went to see them as soon as we returned. I made up a goodie basket with Pimm's, Green and Black's chocolate and Kendal mint cake.

Maggie said, *John and I have given up alcohol and sugar because of health issues.*

I laughed it off, said, *Oh well, you can use them as gifts for other people*, but the nauseous feeling stayed in my belly. There seemed no way I could adequately thank these people.

A few years later, I launched a Kickstarter campaign to help fund my latest run at the Edinburgh Fringe. People from all over the world pledged money. Every time a new backer alert arrived in my inbox, I wanted to shout, *Thank you, thank you, thank you!* But though this effusiveness began from a place of gratitude, it soon turned into a churning, gnawing anxiety. I felt indebted and I wanted to pay them back, mostly, if I am truthful, to get rid of that feeling.

But the constant balancing of the books was in danger of driving me nuts. Does anyone actually know how many thank-yous equal a £20 donation?

I'd already forgotten something I learnt as part of the preparation for my own campaign. Before I launched, I had pledged small amounts to a couple of friends' projects, to see how it felt. At that point, I didn't understand why anyone would want to give me money. But as soon as I pressed the button to donate, I felt a surge of pleasure. It felt delicious to say, *Yes, I can help.*

I can't say what Maggie and John felt. I lost contact with them, to the extent that I can't even remember their surname.

Maybe there's no paying back, no balancing of the books to be done. But, just in case Maggie and John ever see this book…

Thank you.

LOOK! AT HOW I AM HELD

Take gravity.
The perfect amount of push and pull
to both keep my feet on the ground
and allow them to bounce.
And what about oxygen?
Just floating around,
waiting for me to take my next breath.

How about roads?
Once upon a time someone
laid the tarmac and even now
occasionally fixes the potholes.
Others built this café, made this table, these chairs.
And what about the pickers who harvested the tea
currently being dropped into a pot for me?
As for the inventor of the kettle... my hero.
Never mind Edison and his team creating lightbulbs
so I can read my book on this winter afternoon.

I even feel a warm lick in my heart for the council,
or whoever maintains the drains,
so I can flush away my excrement
with one push of a handle.
And the men who clear fatbergs, I love you.
It means the world to me that I don't
have to don a heavy-duty rubber suit
and breathing apparatus
to clamber through slicks of shit and used tampons.

And if I ever felt lonely,
now is not the moment.
I am nothing more
than a temporary nodule
of muscle, bone and fat,
but Tim Berners-Lee gave me the internet.
Okay, not just me, but I have it, whenever I want.

Also almond croissants. And the stars.

So many unseen helpers
nudged me towards this moment.
I raise my cup to them and you,
knowing this poem should never end
but presuming you get the point;

may you also know
how deeply loved you are.
How many and how much
offers itself to everyone,
even you, my fellow nodules
of muscle, bone and fat,
grounded on this speck of a planet,
spun weightless in an infinite universe.

HOW TO KEEP GOING

Today is another invitation.
See the gold lettering?
Your name inked into the space?

Don't worry about what to wear
or how you will get there.
Feel the weight of the card in your hand.

Arm yourself with the secret promise
that you will go home early
if it is the wrong sort of party.

And, if you catch yourself
telling a story that bores
even you? Drop it.

But do turn up.
Whatever the state of your hair.

The party is not the same
without you.

ACKNOWLEDGEMENTS

To Clive and Bridget: thank you for running a superb small press and giving spoken word the space it deserves on bookshelves.

To creative partners old and new: Lucy Ayrton, Rachel Mae Brady, Vera Chok, Kathy Fish, Dan Simpson, Paula Varjack and the Invite Only crew.

For particular help with this collection: Paul Askew, Clare Bold, Rose Condo, Adrian Gillot, Wendy Kaufman, Kieran King, Paul Surman and James Webster.

For excellent website and marketing assistance: Sean Holland and Christian Russell-Pollock at www.joinedupthink.co.uk

For the most beautiful cover design: Lucy Barritt at www.luckybarritt.com

For meticulous copy-editing and subtle editorial suggestions, Harriet Evans.

For organising garden gigs for me to try out new material on their unsuspecting friends during the summer of Covid-19: Mandy Everett, Wendy Gordon, Anki Lucas and Helen Walker.

To Sara and Tony Strong, for friendship and endless support.

For constant inspiration: Rob Bell, Kristin Hanggi and Natalie Roy, Abraham Hicks, Adriene Mishler. You don't know me, but I owe you.

And, of course, Neil. Computer wrangler, design guru, hand holder, irony dispenser, script tickler. Husband.

Lightning Source UK Ltd.
Milton Keynes UK
UKHW011839220621
385973UK00001B/2